Amazon Echo

Become an Alexa and Echo Expert

By Joseph Manuel

expressed or implied. Readers acknowledge that the author is not engaging in the rendering of legal, financial, medical or professional advice.

By reading this document, the reader agrees that under no circumstances are we responsible for any losses, direct or indirect, which are incurred as a result of the use of information contained within this document, including, but not limited to, —errors, omissions, or inaccuracies.

CONTENTS

Introduction

Life is now so hectic that we don't have a single spare minute to sit down and relax. We often find ourselves over burdened with work and in no position to have a breather. Such a lifestyle is obviously not advisable and we need to take matters into our own hands.

The best solution for this problem is to have a personal assistant device that will take your command and finish your work, on or before time. You will feel less burdened about work and do more with your time.

Once you make up your mind to buy a device, you will have a tough time, as there are many assistant devices and software available in the market. However, none of them are as prolific as the Amazon Echo.

It is known that the Amazon Echo is a neat little device that acts as a speaker, and doubles up as a personal assistant. But what are its real uses and how can it help you in your day-to-day life? How does one set it up and start using it? What are the different things to look into before using the Echo? Well, let us find out!

Launched in November 2014, the Echo is now one of the most used voice command devices in the world. Replete with contemporary features, it is a voice command personal assistant.

Through the course of this book, we will look at its aspects, features and various tips and tricks that will help you put your Amazon Echo to good use.

Let us begin.

Chapter 1: What is Amazon Echo?

First and foremost, I thank you for choosing this book and hope you have a good time reading it.

The Amazon Echo is a voice command device that was launched in 2014, in the US. It was their second launch (some might say third after the Fire TV), after the Amazon kindle that was released in 2007.

In this first chapter, we will look at what the device stands for.

What is the Echo?

The Amazon Echo is a speaker cum personal assistant. It is an electronic device that connects to the Internet and helps you perform many day-to-day activities. These include helping you search the Internet and create lists etc. The device is said to have been in the works since 2010 and had a worldwide release in 2015.

The Amazon Echo is like Siri but placed inside a cylindrical speaker. The basic idea is to have a device that can sit in one place in your house and take your commands. This will help make your life easier as a personal assistant will be at your disposal at all times. Amazon came up with the concept of the Echo in order to match Apple's Siri and Microsoft's Cortana. Both of these are personal assistant devices and meant to help you do various things just with the touch of a button.

The Echo goes one level up as you can control it with your voice. Compared to Iron Man's JARVIS, the Echo helps you in many ways. Once you set it up, you will realize that having a handy and sleek voice command assistant at your disposal is one of the best things in the world.

The Amazon Echo is better known as Alexa. It is the device's given name and also the "wake word" you have to use to grab its attention. The name Alexa gives it a personal touch and makes you feel like you are speaking with a real person.

Where can I buy it?

You can buy the Amazon Echo on Amazon.com. The device is easily available and will be shipped within a few days of ordering. As of now, it is only available on the US Amazon website. If you are from another country then you can place an order there and have it delivered to your place. There are many shipping programs to choose from. You can also buy it from a secondary website like eBay if Amazon does not ship to your country. Here is the link to the Amazon Echo. As you can see, it is the number 1 bestseller in home audio speakers on Amazon.

What is its pricing?

The Amazon Echo was launched at a price of $199.99 for regular people and $99 for Amazon prime subscribers. However, the price was dropped by around $20 and is now prices at $179.99. This is a great price for a device that does more than play songs. The personal assistant device will leave you wanting more once you start using it.

What are its uses?

The Amazon Echo can be put to many uses. Right from using it at home to using at the office, the Echo will allow you to perform several functions. We will look at all of them in detail through the course of this book.

These form the basics of the Amazon Echo.

Chapter 2: What Sets the Echo Apart From The Rest

In the previous chapter, we looked at some of the basics of the Amazon Echo and also details of where you can buy it. We also saw that it is often compared to Apple's Siri and Microsoft's Cortana. So, it is now important to understand what sets it apart from these two and why you should choose the Amazon Echo.

Build

The first aspect of the device to look into is its build. The Amazon Echo is a sturdy device that you can use and is made of hard plastic. It is colored black and has many perforations on the outside of the body. While the outsides of the Echo are quite impressive, the insides are even better. Loaded with a DM3725 ARM Cortex-A8 processor and a 256MB LPDDR1 RAM, the device is both powerful and high on capacity. The processor, or CPU, is built into the device and is super-fast. It is also quite smart and will understand your commands well. No wonder it is one of the best Bluetooth speaker devices in the market, and is often referred to as the best personal assistant to own. Top to bottom- the top ring on the Echo is a volume controller, which will help you control the volume of the device. You can turn the ring clockwise to increase the volume and anti-clockwise to decrease it. On top of it are two buttons, one to turn it on, also known as the action button, and the other a mute button! Below this is the reflex pot, which is responsible for creating deeper sounds or enhancing the sound quality. Below that lies a woofer that helps in enhancing the bass quality of the speaker. Right below that is a tweeter that helps in enhancing the high notes. All of these are present inside the body of the Echo. There is a small hole at the bottom, which is for the power LED. This is used to indicate the status of the Wi-Fi. If it remains white then your device is connected, if it is orange then there is no connection, if the orange start to flicker then it indicates that the device is connected with the Wi-Fi but is unable to connect with your Alexa.

Design

The Amazon Echo is a beautiful little device. Standing at a height of 9.25 inches, it is a tiny yet powerful device. Light in weight (1045 grams), it is easy to carry around and will not require you to put in too much effort. The base frame has a diameter of 3.27 inches, which makes it a space saving device. The body is cylindrical in shape and made of metal. That makes the Echo quite a strong device to own. The cylindrical shape of the device makes it easy for you to push the device into any corner of your desk, platform, table etc. You can also push it under the table if you wish to protect it from pets or toddlers.

Speakers

One thing that most gadget savvy people look for is the

quality of the speakers. The speakers need to be great, especially if you wish to use the device a music player. The Amazon Echo comes with an advanced audio distribution profile, which makes it an amazing speaker system. It contains a 2.5 inches woofer and a 2.0-inch tweeter. The former helps in creating a deep audio that focuses on the bass and the latter helps in delivering crisp high notes. There are adequate perforations on the outside of the speaker, which prevent Echoing and allow a crisp and clear sound to escape the device. The multi-directional speaker system produces a 360-degree sound and will immerse your room in no time. Alexa has a crystal clear voice thanks to the echo's speech-unit selection technology. You will be able to hear and understand the device from afar. The sound quality of the Echo is one of the most lauded in the market and what sets it apart from the other similar devices.

Sensors

The sensors or the microphones in the Amazon Echo are concealed yet powerful. They are placed under the light ring on top and are 7 in total. They are spaced equidistant and follow a beam forming technology that makes them quite efficient. There is also one in the center, between the mute and the action button. You can be in any corner of the room and still speak to Alexa with ease. The powerful voice receiving software makes it ideal for people with a soft voice as well. The enhanced voice cancellation feature helps Alexa converse with you even if loud music is being played. This is one of the Echo's most lauded features.

Lighting

The Amazon Echo is a very expressive device. It makes use of lights to tell you what it is up to. There is a light ring on top of the device that surrounds the microphones. This light ring is meant to help you understand certain things, for example, when you switch on Alexa, the light ring will turn white with cyan accents to indicate that the device is switching on. Once done, the lights will go out completely to indicate that the device is now ready to take your command. If the rest of the ring remains dark blue with just one corner being cyan then it indicates that the device is processing your command. When you try to connect to the Wi-Fi, it will start turning clockwise with a bright orange hue and if it successfully connects then it will stabilize, otherwise turn violet. This is an indication that you have to switch the Echo off and turn it on again. If it doesn't work then you have to switch the Wi-Fi on and off. The Echo will cause white light to jump up when you are adjusting the volume and muting it will cause the blue ring to turn completely red.

Privacy

The privacy feature of the Echo is quite unique. You have the chance to mute the device so that it does not record your conversations. This makes it ideal for all those that wish to have private conversations with the people in the room. Don't worry; you don't have to switch off the device every time. Simply pressing the mute button will do the trick. But remember to unmute your Alexa if you wish to resume using it as usual.

Cloud storage

The Amazon Echo has a cloud storage feature. Whatever you speak with your Echo is all recorded and stored in the cloud. You can login to your account and access it at any time and from anywhere. All your songs and other data will also be stores, thereby giving you an additional back up facility for all your important files.

Usage

The Amazon Echo is very easy to use! Right from children to housewives and working professionals, everybody will find it easy to operate the Amazon Echo. They won't have to go through pains to set it up and will be able to do so with ease. We will look at the different components to expect with your Echo and setting it up, in the following chapter.

These form some of the important features of the Echo and what makes the device such a hit amongst the users. These features are often used to compare with the other similar software.

Chapter 3: Getting Started With Your Amazon Echo

In the previous chapter, we looked at some of the basic features of the Echo and in this one, we will look at the components that you will receive with the device and how you can set it up.

What to expect with your Echo

Your Amazon Echo is a speaker device and will come with the following components.

The speaker

This is the main device that we are talking about. We looked at the various features of the speaker in the previous chapter including its build and design features. This is the main component in the Echo box.

A power adaptor/ cable

The power adaptor cable is what will help you connect your Amazon Echo to a power source. It is a 6 feet long cable that will help you place it anywhere in the room. You can buy a longer cord for your device if you like and place the device in the right place.

A starter guide

All devices come with a starter guide and so does your Amazon Echo. The start guide will run you through the basics of the device and how you can set it up. You can go through this guide once to understand the different features of your device and also fill out the warranty forms.

A remote (sold separately)

The Amazon Echo remote is a neat device. It provides you with the basic functions of controlling the volume, muting and fast forward/ rewind and play. It connects with your speaker via Bluetooth. There is a small microphone present on top of the remote that allows you to converse with Alexa. You have to place it close to your mouth and speak into and Alexa will be able to hear you. This is a great feature for those that wish to control the device from a different room. The remote works on 2 AAA batteries and you can pair a single remote with your device at one time. It comes with a magnetic strip that you can use to stick the remote anywhere you like. Remember that you don't have to say the "wake word" while speaking into the remote, as Alexa will automatically take your command. The remote is sold separately on the Amazon website.

The Amazon Echo app

The amazon echo app is a must for you if you wish to control your Alexa with ease. As you know, the echo is a physical device and sits pretty on your desk or table. Some might thing that is a little limiting and will not allow you to control the device on the move. But this is just a misconception. You can control Alexa by using the app.

The app can be downloaded on your phone, tablet or computer. It is available on the app store, the windows store and also the iOS store. It is free to download and the size of the application varies across the different platforms. It can be between 711.6KB and 936.4KB. Here are some of the functions of the Alexa app.

It helps in acting as an account authenticator. You will be able to connect with your device through the app.

- You can connect Wi-Fi with your Alexa.
- You can navigate the Bluetooth devices in your area and connect them with your Alexa.
- Avail information of the tasks that are now running.
- Control the music that is playing. You can play it, pause it, rewind it, fast-forward it, choose the next one, stop the music, resume the music, restart it etc.
- Get Alexa to send copies of the different files to your app.
- Change up the **Settings** of your Alexa.
- You can keep the device going and prevent it from going to sleep.

These are just some of the features and there are many more that you will understand once you start using the app.

The home screen of the app is quite simple. You will be able to see all the recent requests that you have, an option to browse through the different conversations that you have had with Alexa, many links to Internet sites,

Setting up your Echo

Here are the steps you need to follow to set up your Amazon Echo.

Start by plugging in the adaptor cable to the echo. Plug the other end into a power source. Now press the action button for a few seconds and wait for Alexa to start up.

Next, connect the device to Wi-Fi. There are three steps to undertake to connect the app with your amazon echo. First, you can open the app and connect with your amazon echo. For this, open the app and go to **Settings** and select the Update Wi-Fi option. If you wish to add another echo then you can choose the Set up a new Echo option.

The next method is to press the action button until it turns orange. Then, a list of available Wi-Fi networks will appear on your app. You can choose the one you wish to connect with.

Next, you can choose the Wi-Fi network and type in the password. Once done, the echo will change color to a stable white.

The next step is to add your location so that Alexa can detect where you are accessing it. Doing so will help you in many ways and is one of the important new features of the echo.

The next step is to choose a date format. You can pick the date and the time format that you would like to maintain with your amazon echo.

The next step is to customize your app. You can go to the **Settings** on your app and choose the different **Settings** that you wish to maintain with your echo.

Next, you should pair your remote with your Alexa.

Pairing remote

To pair your remote with your Alexa, start by adding in the batteries by pulling away the battery door. Now go to your

Alexa app and pick the navigation menu on the left. Select the setting and choose *Pair Remote*. Your remote is now paired and ready to use. You can also select the *Forget Remote* if you wish to pair a new remote. You can also have your Bluetooth on and the device will detect the remote in no time.

Connectivity

Your Alexa will pair up with a whole array of devices. We already saw how you can connect it with the remote; now let us look at some other devices that you can connect the speaker with.

Fire OS

You can connect with any device that runs on the fire operating system. So, your fire phone, fire tablets and also fire TV can all be connected with Alexa. But these have to be running on fire 2.0 or above in order to pair with Alexa.

Android

The next platform is android. You can connect with all your devices that run on android 4 and above. You can upgrade to it and then connect with your Alexa.

IOS

You can use the Alexa with iOS 7.0 and above. This includes phones, tablets and also computers.

You can create a group for all and have access to all through one place. For this, you can go to **Settings**> Groups > Select Group. You can choose a name for it like Home Group or Office Group and add in all the specific devices.

Creating profiles

The amazon echo is a smart little device. It will allow you to create multiple profiles that will each belong to a particular family member. Here are the steps to follow for the same.

- First, ensure that the person creating the profile is present in the room with you.
- Next, access your app and go to the **Settings** that are present in the left panel.
- Now choose the Household Profiles that is present there.
- Now Alexa will ask questions in regard to the second person and they will have to type in the password and answers to the questions.
- Once done, Alexa will maintain two different accounts. You can add as many as 4 profiles or more depending on the space available.

You can also remove a person from your household if you like. Here are the steps to adopt for it.

- Go to the left panel in the app and choose the **Settings** option.
- Under the Account option, pick Manage Your Amazon Household.
- Now select 'Remove' that is present next to the profile that you wish to delete.
- Now pick Remove from Household to confirm your move.
- This will remove the person from the list.

You can easily switch up the profiles as well. Here is how you can do so.

- Start by saying Switch accounts.
- Now access the app and choose the profile you wish to pick.

- If you wish to check which profile you are on currently then ask: which profile is this?

This is the easiest and best way to maintain different files on your Alexa and keep them from intermingling.

Chapter 4: Using The Amazon Echo At Home

Till now, we looked at the different aspects of the Amazon Echo. Now, we will look at some of the practical uses of the device at home.

Accessing Internet

The most important role of the Amazon Echo is helping you access the Internet. In this day and age, where everything is connected via wires, it becomes extremely important for you to have a device that allows instant access to the Internet. Gone are the days when you held bulky cellphones in your hand to access the Internet. The Amazon Echo will help you connect to the Internet with the snap of a finger. All you have to do is wake up your Alexa and ask the machine to search the web. It will do so in a matter of seconds and read out the results. Isn't that simply superb?

Accessing Wikipedia

It is a well-known fact that Wikipedia is one of the most

searched websites in the world. You can look for any information you like. And with your Amazon Echo, the job becomes much easier! All you have to do is give your Alexa the command and it will take care of the rest. You can get the machine to read from a particular paragraph, a particular line, repeat it etc. This is an important feature of the Echo and sure to be a hit with every single person in your family.

To-do lists

Have you always wanted to maintain a to-do list that you can refer and go about your routine? Have you wanted a device that will take down the things to do for you? Well, your search ends here. With the Amazon Echo, it is extremely easy for you to prepare to-do lists. All you have to do is call out to Alexa and ask her to add to your *to-do* list. Alexa will take care of the rest. You can also ask the machine to tick off the different items as soon as they are done. You can get Alexa to mail the list to you as well.

Shopping lists

It is just as easy for you to create shopping lists. All you have to do is get Alexa to create the list for you. You can shout out the different things you wish to buy and Alexa will record them in a list. You can then get her to mail the list to you so that you can access it from anywhere and any device. Once you are done with the shopping, you can ask Alexa to delete it for you. What's more, you can maintain the list and get Alexa to send a copy to you at any time.

School planner

You can take the help of Alexa to plan your child's school schedule. Parents will find it easy to know when a certain test or exam is coming up. They will also find it easy to maintain an event schedule. This schedule will tell them when an event is coming up, like an exam and start preparing for it. Again, you can get Alexa to mail it to you, so that you can have a copy of it ready with you.

Music

The next best use of Alexa is to listen to your favorite music. Some people will want this at the top of the list, as the Echo is after all a speaker device. How will it feel to have your favorite songs play automatically as soon as you entered the house? Will it not better your mood instantly to have a soothing song play after a day of hard work? Well, all you have to do is create a playlist and ask Alexa to play the songs. The machine will automatically start playing them one after the other. You can get it to stop by giving the stop music command. This is a great way to fall asleep at night.

Recipes

For all the novice cooks out there, the ultimate kitchen helper is on the way! The Amazon Echo will prove to be one of the best helpers that you can have in your kitchen. All you have to do is give the command and the Echo will look for a recipe for you. You can set it up in your kitchen and have everything laid out in front of you. As soon as Echo starts reading out the recipe, you can start preparing the dishes. You can also stop Alexa at any time and then get it to repeat something for you.

Planner

How would it feel to have someone help you plan a holiday or an event? Whether it is a business trip or a leisure trip, all you have to do is get Alexa to make a note of the itinerary. You can also take its help to plan a party. You can get the device to make a party guest list, a to-do list, a shopping list etc. All in all, you will have a fun time with your Amazon

Echo and won't feel like planning a party or a trip without it.

Control lights/ devices

It is now easy for you to control, dim and turn off lights and other devices in your house by making use of Amazon Echo. All you have to do is connect all of them together and then command them by voice to do as you say. This is great for elders that cannot walk up to the switch and also for parents who want to control the lights in their child's room. You can also use the feature to switch off all the lights in your house when you are leaving to go out.

These form the different ways in which you can use the Amazon Echo at home. But it is not limited to just these uses. There can be many more and you will only know them once you start using the device.

Chapter 5: Using The Amazon Echo At Office

Apart from home use, you can also use the Amazon Echo at office. Once you start using it, you will see how it helps you finish all your work with much ease. Let us look at the Echo's practical uses in this chapter.

Organizing

The first and most important use of the Amazon Echo in your office is that it helps in your organizational practices. You can link all the different office software together. Right from email to Google calendar and other such office suites, you can unite and link with your Echo. You will have a simple and pleasurable experience with the Echo. You can treat the device as your assistant and ask to reply to emails, set meeting reminders etc. You can easily increase your productivity and do more in less time.

Editing

Editing is now a breeze with the Amazon Echo. You will have

the chance to edit many documents with ease. You can feed the data to your computer and then get Alexa to read it out loud. You can also have the text in front of you. As Alexa reads it, you can sit back and relax to it and if you notice something wrong then you can stop Alexa immediately. You can correct the error then and there. You can again get Alexa to resume and read out the text. This is great for editors as they can edit more in less time. 5

Calculating

If you are bad at math and can't add numbers fast enough, then you can use the Echo you help you out. All you have to do is read out the different numbers and then ask Alexa to add them. Alexa will quickly tell you the sum. This is great when you are calculating big numbers and don't have the patience to type the numbers out on a calculator. You will see that your work has reduced considerably and are able to prepare reports and other documents requiring statistical calculations with ease.

Assistant at meetings

How will it be to have an assistant follow you into the meeting room and take down notes? Now, with the Amazon Echo, you can have the assistant follow you, take notes and save it for future reference! All you have to do is carry your Echo to the meeting room, set it up and start recording everything. Once everything is recorded, you can play it and refer back to it. You can also carry it along to help with presentations. You can get Alexa to preside over the meeting and speak in lieu of you. That will make your office life a breeze!

Waiting Instructions

Sometimes, you might be out of the office and your

customers might have to wait in the waiting room. In such a case, you can get Alexa to speak with them and give them instructions. You can type in the text that you want Alexa to read out to your waiting customers. In fact, you can also entertain your waiting guests by asking Alexa to play songs from a list. You can choose some classical tunes that will keep the customers interested in sitting in the office instead of leaving.

Buying music

It is quite easy for you to buy or download music from Amazon. All you have to do is ask Alexa to download the album from the store. You will have to remain logged into your account in order to do so. Once Alexa finds what you are looking for, it will ask you for a code. You can use the code to buy the music and will have to be chosen while setting up the device. This step is needed to prevent random people from buying from your account and charging you. As soon as the album is downloaded, Alexa will start playing the songs automatically. You can also connect with Spotify and other such sites and start playing the songs. You can also select the 1-click setting that will help you purchase the music through a payment account that you have linked.

Leaving ratings

Many times, we feel lazy to leave behind rating on websites such as Amazon. In such a case, you can get Alexa to leave behind a message in lieu of you. Whether it is an album or a product that you have purchased, you can ask Alexa to leave behind a star rating of your choice. You can also get Alexa to leave behind a review.

WeMo/ SmartThings/ Insteon/ Wink/ Philips He

You can have all the lights in your office connected via

WeMo, SmartThings, Insteon, Wink and Philips Hue, and switch off all the lights and other electricals in your office with just a command. This is especially useful if you are the last person out of the office and want to switch off all the lights together from the door. You can also switch off the humidifier, the a/c and all other devices that are connected with your Echo.

IFTTT

If this then that is a great little tool that you can use to connect all the different apps together. There are many that you can connect and avail benefits from. You can do a quick search and look up the best ones to connect. Some of the best IFTTT recipes include Instagram, Flickr, readability etc.

Supplies

Now you will never have to order the different supplies in your office manually. All you have to do is maintain a list and then get Alexa to order everything for you. Whether it is a set of bulbs or stationary or even music, you can order everything with much ease. If you wish to remove something from the list then you can simply delete it or ask Alexa to do it herself.

These form the different ways in which the Amazon Echo will help you at office. Again, it isn't limited to just these. The other uses will reveal themselves as and when you use the device.

Chapter 6: Using The Amazon Echo With Children

There are many uses for Amazon Echo. It is like the list is endless and you can do many things with it. One such utility is to use the Echo to teach your child or help them with their mundane activities. Let us look at what you can do with it.

Projects

It is almost a nightmare for any child to finish a project on time and get good grades. But now, with the Amazon Echo, you can help your child finish the project easily. As you know, it is easy for you to look for anything on the Internet. You can search for the topic and get Alexa to read it out. Your child can then write it down. What's more, you can connect it with your printer and get Alexa to print out any pictures and photos that your child might need for his or her project. Projects and home works will now be a breeze thanks to your Amazon Echo.

Revising

Does your child pester you to take his or her test before an exam? Do you wish to have a ready teacher that will help take the test? Well, the Amazon Echo will help you in that department. All you have to do is get your child to write down the answers to the questions and ask Alexa to read out from the original text. That way, your child can do a self-test. If your child has written something wrong then you can ask him or her to revise it once again.

Reminders

You can help your child set a reminder on the Echo. The Echo will then remind you about the event. But you have to remember that you can only set an alarm the previous day and not any time before that. You have to tell your child about the same and ask them to set the alarm 24 hours prior.

Alarms

You can now easily set alarms with your Amazon Echo. You can get the Echo to wake your child up at the same time every day. It is especially useful before an exam as your child can get up early and revise. But the same previous rule applies here too. You can only set an alarm the previous day and not any time before that. If you do, then Alexa will forget about it just like you would. You have to teach your child the same.

Games

The Alexa can be used to play many games. Right from rock paper scissors to crosswords, there are many games that you can play with the Echo. Alexa is very interactive and will respond to you promptly. Many times, Alexa also suggests a game to you based on your mood. You can teach your child to play these games with Alexa and they will have hours of fun with it.

Discipline

It will be quite easy for you to discipline your child. As you know, you can make use of the remote to speak into the Amazon Echo from afar. You can make use of the same to speak to your child from a different room. Now imagine that your child is not doing his homework, you can leave him or her in a room with Alexa and then speak into the remote. You have to say; *Simon says* and then, recite what you want Alexa to say. It can be anything like, "no playing until you finish your homework". Your child will actually think that Alexa is speaking and disciplining him or her. This will of course work only until your child understands how the remote works.

Bedtime reminder

You can now help your child sleep on time. You can get your child to ask Alexa how long before bedtime, so that they can sleep on time. Alexa will reply back with the exact time left before they should hit the bed. You can set the alarm for them and help them get into bed on time every day. Again, you can make use of the discipline technique to put them to bed.

Bedtime stories

How wonderful would it be for your child if a bedtime story were read out to him or her on a daily basis? Of course, given our hectic lives, we will not be able to so. However, now with the Amazon Echo, you can have a bedtime story read out to your child! You can download audio books from the Amazon store and get Alexa to read it out for your child. This will ensure that your child falls asleep and will also help in improving his or her thinking capacity. You can choose a different book every night and get Alexa to read automatically for your child without you being present.

White noise

You can also get Alexa to play something soothing like white noise to help your child sleep better. White noise is known to help people avail a good night's sleep and your child too can sleep peacefully. You can use the remote to instruct Alexa or teach your child to switch it on.

These form the various ways in which the Amazon Echo can help your child. You can allow your child to explore the other uses.

Chapter 7: Echo updates 2015

The amazon echo experienced a slew of new updates in October 2015. These updates are meant to make your device much more efficient than it already is. Here are the different new features of the product.

Yelp

Now, amazon echo will allow you to add your location. Adding in your location will help you find things around you with ease. This can include looking for local restaurants, movie theatres, super markets etc. To get started with this, go to the **Settings** on the Alexa app and then select your device from there. You can add in your address. Once done, Alexa will store it. Now say you are looking for an Indian restaurant, you can say, "Alexa, find an Indian restaurant close by". Alexa will take your command and find one for you.

Audible

Your Alexa now pairs up with audible to read out audio books for you. You can have Alexa read them out to you and also your children. You can download audio books from kindle and then get audible to read it out for you. It is also compatible with Whispersync, which will allow you to pause the book and then restart from the same word. This is a new feature and was not available before. You can get Alexa to read the book one after another tirelessly.

Google calendars

Some people would complain about amazon not being able to connect with Google apps. But this problem is now solved! You can successfully link to your Google calendar and search for any event. You can also look up the event and prepare for it. You can go to the **Settings** in your Alexa app and link your Google calendar. You can then ask Alexa if an event is on its way.

Shop

Shopping is now made extremely easy. You can maintain a shopping list on your Amazon account and access it from anywhere and at any time. You can place the same order again or edit it out. You can also get Alexa to read it out for you and get the machine to delete some of the things from the list. For example, you can say, "Alexa, read me my shopping list". Alexa will start reading out the different items on the list. If you want it to kick something out then you can ask Alexa to delete it from your list before placing the order on amazon.com.

Traffic

How nice would it be if someone read out the easiest route that you could take to reach a place? Not only can you reach on time but also save on having to go through a lot of traffic. You can feed two or three routes in and then get Alexa to pick the best one for you. Then, you can ask, "Alexa how is the traffic on the route?" You will be able to avoid a route if there is a lot of traffic there and can settle for one that is less crowded. To set this up, you can go to the **Settings** on the Alexa app and then choose Traffic. You can fill in the *From* and *To* fields and then save the changes. You can also add in stops on the way by picking the New Stop option.

News

Are you the type that loves to be informed about the news at all times? Do you like knowing what is happening around you and remain well informed about current affairs and events? Then Alexa will surely help you out with that. You can get Alexa to read out whatever is present in your flash briefing. All you have to say is, "Alexa, read me what's in my flash briefing" and Alexa will take care of it. You can also simply ask what the news is, and have it read out. You can also pause it, stop it or go to the previous news if you like.

Weather

It is important to get weather updates from time to time, especially if you live in a region where it rains or snows often. You can ask Alexa what the weather will be like. You can ask about the weather on the same day or in the days to come. For this, you will have to go to the **Settings** and then add in your address. Alexa will have instant access to the weather conditions and tell you about it.

Sports

If you are a sports fan and wish to have sports updates, then you can have them on a minute-to-minute basis. This is especially great if a game is on and you wish to have a constant commentary. You can use the sports update feature for this function. Some of the different events that Alexa covers include the MLB, MLS, NHL, NFL WNBA and NBA.

The choice is yours and you can pick one, all or several.

Music

You can now connect to many radio stations with much ease. You can connect with Spotify or Pandora and start listening to your favorite tunes. You can also access Prime Music, which is an ad free access that amazon provides to its users. You can listen from a versatile library. You can also request for a particular music that you are in the mood for. All you have to say is, Alexa, play me some Jazz music and it will do the rest.

Tones

Now forget waking up to the same old tunes! There are a few new tones now for you to choose from. These can be your reminder tones, your alarm tones etc. The new ones will help you wake up on time and dance to! There are some peppy ones and also some mellow ones that love to wake up to sweet music.

Multiple timers, reminders

It is now possible for you to set multiple alarms and reminders, which was not possible before. You don't have to worry about Alexa replacing an alarm with another. There is space for you to keep many alarms and reminders without having to replace them.

Wink/ Insteon

The amazon echo was able to pair with WeMo and Philips hue bulbs but now, it will also pair with Wink and Insteon. You will be able to control the lights and other devices in your house with ease. You don't have to rely on the app anymore and can switch off lights, open garage doors, switch off the heater all just by calling it out. You can link all of them by going to the **Settings** and picking the individual options.

These are the new updates that the amazon echo received. But updation is an ongoing process and there will be more such that will make its way from time to time.

Chapter 8: Training And Maintaining Your Echo

In this chapter of the book, we will look at how you can train your amazon echo and also clean it.

Training the echo

It is important to train the amazon echo. The amazon echo is a smart device no doubt, but you have to train it in order to improve its functioning.

Here are the steps you have to take for it.

- Start by opening the amazon echo app.
- Now go to the navigation panel and select the Voice Training option.
- Now choose Start.
- Now speak a phrase of your choice into the app.
- You have to maintain a normal tone and voice.
- Once done, pick the Next option to speak the next phrase.

- If you wish to cancel and repeat it again, then pick Pause and Repeat Phrase.
- To end a session, then choose Pause and End Session.

You can pick as many phrases as you like and try to incorporate as many different words in it as possible.

You have to sit in a comfortable position while giving the voice training to your Alexa. You have to sit or stand in the position that you would normally stand in. remember to not use the voice remote while training your Alexa as it might confuse the device.

You have to get each family member to speak to the device in order for it to identify everyone. This will also help Alexa not take commands from voices that it does not identify.

Remember that your echo will get better with time. It will get accustomed to your vocabulary and also voice quality.

Wake word

Before we look at the how you can train your Alexa, we will look at the wake word first. The wake word refers to the word that you will be using to address your amazon echo. As we already saw, most people prefer to name the device Alexa, which is also the company's given name. But if you wish to use something else then you can do so by changing the name. For this, go to the **Settings** and choose the Wake Word option. There, you can type in the name of your choice. There is a default name available there, which is Simon. You can choose something simple like Amazon to be the wake word as it will be easy to remember and use. You have to use this wake word to wake the device up if it falls asleep.

Safety precautions

Remember that your Alexa when paired with the different

devices in your house will take command and do as you say. This means that anybody who accesses your devices can get Alexa to do what they want. If you have any of your doors connected to the device and get Alexa to open or close it, then you have to protect these devices. If they fall into the wrong hands then they can be misused. It is important that you get alerts about any device that was operated through Alexa. You should also take care to disable Alexa before you leave town.

Cleaning

It is important to clean and maintain your echo. If you live in a dusty area or a humid one then you will have to clean your echo from time to time. Here are some things that you can do to clean the echo.

- Start by using a blower to blow out any dust that might have settled inside the speaker. You can either use the blower attachment or a compressed air can for this purpose.
- Next, you can add a few drops of liquid soap or fabric detergent to a cup of warm water and dissolve it.
- Now use a small piece of sponge or cloth and dip it into the solution.
- You have to squeeze out all the excess water from it.
- Now wipe the outsides of the speaker and loosen any dust and dirt.
- If there are any tough stains then you can use a toothbrush to loosen and clean it.
- Once done, you can place the speaker in open air for it to dry.
- You should also clean the cord thoroughly. You can use the same solution for it.

- It is best to clean your device once a month to protect it from dust and dirt.
- But don't try to open the device to clean it. You might not be able to put it back together again. If there is something stuck inside then you will have to take it to be serviced.

Chapter 9: Problems With Your Echo

When it comes to a new device, it is important that you know its benefits and also its pitfalls. No device is perfect and your Alexa has a few shortcomings that are discussed in this chapter.

Unsatisfactory results

One problem that many people have with their echo is that the results it throws up are not really satisfactory. If you are looking for a good Italian restaurant nearby, then it might simply end up reading from a random website names of restaurants that don't even exist anymore. This can be quite a bit of a problem for all those that wish to have accurate results, like what they will have if they searched for it themselves. This might stem from the fact that the echo will take into consideration GPS settings

Accent

One complaint that most new owners will have with the echo is its inability to identify your accent. This is especially pertinent with those that have a heavy accent like Australian or India. Alexa is mostly accustomed to the American accent. So, it might misunderstand you and give you a result that is different from what you are looking for. You also might have to speak in an American accent, which might seem a bit cumbersome. However, with regular use, Alexa will be able to understand you better. You will also learn to speak in a way that helps the device understand you well.

Language

With more and more devices allowing people to pick a language of their choice, the echo lags behind. Communication with the device is only available in English and not any other language. This is seen as a bit of a problem for all those who wish to use the device but cannot make sense of English. Maybe this feature will be worked upon in the future but right now, it's a drawback.

Price

Some people complain about the price of the device being too high. They think that the $179.99 that the speaker comes at is a bit too much and it is a waste of money to spend so much on something that is available for less than $100. But they don't realize that it is not just a speaker and comes with many other features that make it a little personal assistant.

Remote

One cause of concern now is the unavailability of the remote. It seems to have been sold out on the amazon website and the ones available on other sites like eBay are quite expensive. So if you were to look for one to buy then you would have to shell out a lot more money than what people before you bought it for. This can be a big problem to those that are already complaining about the high price of the echo.

Homophone issues

The Alexa suffers from a homophones issue. Homophones refer to words that have two or more meanings. For example, desert can refer to both a sweet dish and leaving someone or something. You might be aiming for the former but Alexa might give you a result for the latter. So, this can be a problem if you are seriously looking for something important and Alexa throws up the wrong result. But amazon is said to be working on this issue to fix it.

Search engine

Another problem might be that of Alexa not picking Google to search for your results. It will randomly scour the web for your results and might pick something that is not your ideal choice. This will be a problem as Google or Bing usually lists the best results and going to some other search engine might not cut it for you.

Reminders/ alarms

As you know, you can set an alarm only 24 hours before the event. This can be a problem. You might forget about it just the day before and then end up forgetting about it altogether. That is not something you want, especially if it is to do with an exam or a test. So, you will have to develop the habit of setting an alarm 24 hours before in order to be on the safer side. You can set both a reminder and an alarm so that at least one of them reminds you about the event successfully.

Weight

As you know, the amazon echo weighs in at a mere 1045 grams, which some might say is a bit too light. It can be easily knocked off the table and damaged. This is especially likely if you have pets or children that might knock it over. You will have to be extra careful with it in that case.

Unavailability

One of the biggest problems with the amazon echo is the unavailability of the device. It is not available on all amazons across the world and is mostly exclusively available only on the US site. This will make it a bit tough for you to find one easily. You might have to ask someone returning from the US to get it for you. They are available on eBay but it might take a long time for the seller to ship it to you. However, it is now available on many local country amazons.

These form some of the issues that might come with your amazon echo.

Chapter 10: General Echo Tips and Tricks

Here are a few tips and tricks that you can follow in order to use your Echo optimally. These will help you put your Amazon Echo to maximum use.

Updates

You have to scan for updates from time to time in order to have the latest one installed on your echo. Your device will automatically loom for these updates every night and install them automatically. But you can also do a search to look for them. It is best to have the latest installed in order to avail all the benefits. The CPU will be up to date and might download software that will help increase its efficiency. You can manually update your Alexa by pressing the mute button and allow it to stand for 30 minutes or so. Once done, you will see that your Alexa has updated.

Help

If at any time you need help with your Alexa then you can

open up this book and have your doubt cleared. You can also turn to this <u>Site</u> and avail help. You can also use the community forum to ask and have your questions answered. There are also many questions that have already been asked on the echo on the amazon echo page on amazon.com. You can also call amazon up and ask them about your warranties and other such questions. There are also instructional videos that are easily available on sites like YouTube, which will help you understand the different features of the device.

Warranties

You will have to look into the warranty details as soon as you get the device. It will be important for you to understand what the company will cover and what it will not. Once you understand them, you can fill out the forms. There is the amazon echo 1 year-limited warranty and also the warranty on the remote. You can read all the terms and conditions <u>Here</u>. You should also read the notices and understand everything that there is to in order to use your echo the right way.

Resetting the echo

As you know, it is important to reset all your electronic devices from time to time. Resetting helps the device to work efficiently. In order to reset your amazon echo, you can use a paper clip or even a small pin. You can find the reset button near the power adaptor at the base of the device. You have to press it for a few seconds. When you do so, the light ring on top will first turn orange and then blue to indicate that it has been reset. The light will then switch off and on again and display the orange color. Now open the app and connect to the Wi-Fi network once again. Your device is now successfully reset.

Deleting recordings

If you wish to delete the recordings from your clod then it is quite easy to do so. You can login to your account and access the history by going to the **Settings** page. There, you can either choose to delete all of the recordings in bulk or choose and pick the ones that you don't want to keep. Doing so will help you increase the space and will also allow you to delete any important conversations, like password discussions, that Alexa might have recorded.

Easter eggs

There are many Easter eggs that are available with your Alexa. These refer to fun answers that your Alexa will know to random questions. Some of them include How tall is president Obama or who lives in a pineapple under the sea. Alexa now also answers Star Wars questions. There are many other questions that you can ask and have answered. You can do a quick Internet search to find the others. You and Alexa can have hours of fun!

These form the tips and tricks that will help you use your echo better.

Key Highlights

The very first thing to understand here is the meaning of the Amazon Echo. As you now know, it is a speaker cum personal assistant that is run by voice command. Don't mistake it for a blue tooth speaker that takes your command to play songs alone. It will do a lot more than just that. It is a personal secretary of sorts and will help you do many things on a daily basis

The design and build of the device is both ingenious beautiful. It is a small device that stands at 9.25 inches and made of metal with a black matte finish. It contains both woofers and sub-woofers that will help produce a clear sound. The device contains 7 microphones that are extremely powerful and will pick up voice signals from anywhere in the room. The speakers produce a crisp sound with emphasis on bass and pitch.

Your device comes with a remote, an adaptor and also a start-up guide. Setting up your Echo is quite easy. You can go through the guide if you like or through this book once again. Anybody can set it up including children and elders. You might have to help them with the pairing and then they will be good to go.

You can connect your device to many external devices including the remote, android, iOS and fire OS devices. But they have to be running on versions 4.0 and above, 7.0 and above and 2.0 and above respectively. You can update your systems to these if you wish to pair them with your Alexa. The remote is easy to pair with your Alexa. It can be paired using blue tooth or through the app.

We looked at the different uses that you can avail by setting up your Alexa at home. Right from helping you prepare shopping lists to playing your favorite music automatically, Alexa will do many things for you. Your life will start getting simpler and you will do many things in less time. But don't limit yourself to just the uses mentioned in this book and explore other uses as well.

The Amazon Echo finds many uses in the office. You can do many things including organizing the different office suites, buying music online, ordering supplies online, leaving behind ratings, connecting with WeMo, Philips hue, SmartThings etc. Your productivity will increase and you will do more in less time. Your office life will never be the same again once you start using the Amazon Echo!

We also looked at how you can use the Amazon Echo to teach and train your children. They will have the chance to do their homework on time, know how long before bedtime, revise for a test, play games and also have bedtime stories read out. There are many other things that your child can do by using the Amazon Echo. Just set it up in their room and let them have an amazing time.

There are many updates that were introduced in October 2015. These updates make the Echo extremely efficient and will also increase your efficiency. We looked at the different new updates and you can avail them on your device.

The Echo app is meant to help you connect with your Amazon Echo with ease. You can download it on any of your devices that run on the specific platforms. Once you download the app, you can follow the steps mentioned in this book to set up your Alexa.

It is important for you to maintain your Amazon Echo. It is best to clean it from time to time. You can make use of the blower function to blow the dust and dirt out. You can then make use of some disinfectant liquid to dissolve in water and use a sponge to clean the outside of the device. Once done, you can place it in an open-air atmosphere for it to dry. You have to clean the chords as well and remove any sticky build up over it. The remote can be easily cleansed making use of a wet sponge followed by a dry sponge.

It is important to know some of the pitfalls of the device. There are a few issues with the device that you should be aware of and they were mentioned in this book. It is only fair that you consider them while buying the Echo and understand that no device can be perfect. But Amazon promises to tackle these issues and perfect the device for you. You will have to be patient until such time and keep updating your device from time to time.

We looked at many tips and tricks that you can use with your Amazon Echo and increase its efficiency. But given how the software keeps changing, you have to be prepared to adapt to the changes. You can also look for tips and tricks on the Internet and better your experience with the device.

Should you have any doubt about your amazon echo, and then you can look at some help videos. You can also have your doubts cleared by asking questions on the community. The best place to ask questions is on the amazon echo page on amazon.com.

You have to understand that the Amazon Echo betters with age. This means that it will work well with time. It will get accustomed to your speech, commands, voice recognition, grammar etc. The more you use your Echo, the better it performs. You will get used to the machine within a week's time and not be able to live without it after that!

Conclusion

I thank you once again for choosing this book and hope you had a good time reading it.

The main aim of this book was to educate you on the purpose and importance of using the Amazon Echo on a day-to-day basis.

The information mentioned in this book is all meant to help you get started with your Echo and put it to good use.

As you can see, the device is quite simple to set up and even easier to use. You will see that it is decreasing the effort that you exert towards performing your routine activities.

The device is a great gift idea and can be gifted to anybody who loves electronic gadgets. It can also be gifted to children, as it greatly helps in their daily activities.

You can also give it to your parents or elders and help them lead an easy life.

All in all, the Amazon Echo is a great little device that you can buy and bring home lots of happiness.

All the best!

Recommended Reading

Amazon Echo: Users Guide & Manual To Amazon Echo: Secret Tips And Tricks To Connect You To The World

hyperurl.co/echo

51612406R00033

Made in the USA
Lexington, KY
01 May 2016